Love: Fearless Hearts

Embrace your Ego
Free your Soul

Neale Daniel

First edition 7th September 2014.

ISBN 978-1-291-98855-0 Paperback

Cover design by Divine Inspiration!

Published by Neale Daniel.
Printed by www.lulu.com

Contents

Introduction

Having spent decades battling with my ego and acquiring
wisdom from many of the world's traditions. I kept coming
back to the same question. Why is it so difficult to develop
your consciousness? I felt as if I was stuck repeating the
same lessons. I perceived that it should be simple, easily
accessible and obvious.

In this the second book of the Love: series, I share an
alternative approach to transform your ego into your
greatest asset. It builds upon our innate skills as actors to
perform our divine personality, from our heart space. The
ego does not fight this creation it simply observes. The
created divine personality eventually takes over, all with
little effort, it just happens. The result is that you become
your true self. Free from fears.
Easy Peasy!

Neale Daniel.   5th July 2014

Terminology

The terms 'ego' and 'spirit self' mean many things. To simplify this book I have rolled several characteristics together under these names. Not linguistically accurate, but it does make for a less complex explanation.

Spirit self:
All your spiritual facets. Your higher self, divine self, spark of source, spirit and soul.

Ego:
Your personality, identity, conscious mind and unconscious mind. The Earthly non-physical aspects of your body.

Physical self:
Living flesh and bones.

I
Love

The beginning

What are we?

We are a divine soul, a being of unselfish love and oneness with all. An aspect of the divine source.

We are infinite, we have no beginning or end and this means that we are continuously growing and expanding.

Our growth is through a process of what we would describe as new experiences.

We are spirit beings

Tricky to describe;

A spark of the Divine
In-Unity
Connected to all
Spirit
Love
Infinite
Indestructible
Eternal
No physical form
Shapeless
Flowing

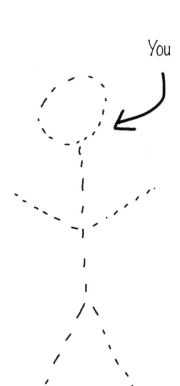

You

Human form

Here on Earth we spirit beings inhabit a physical body, we are conscious energy that is associated with the body, we do not actually occupy it as a driver would a car. However I will portray our physical body as containing our spirit for simplicity.

We consist of three layers
1/ Spirit self
2/ Ego
3/ Physical self

Ego software

The ego is an unusual thing and problematic
to describe, there is nothing tangible. Unlike
your eternal spirit it is finite and fleeting.
When you die the ego ceases to exist. The
body remains and the spirit departs.

The ego is thought, it is neither spirit nor
physical. The ego is like the program running
on a computer, your personal software.

The ego is not a 'thing' but a way of doing
things, it directs your body's operation.

This temporary ego controls your physical
life and acts as a thought membrane
between your physical and spiritual aspects.

Experience

We spirits are experiencing this lifetime on Earth as a passenger in this unique physical body.

Our physical body is directed by the ego which allows us to experience being a separate physical individual with the creative opportunities for new experiences that it provides.

Our deep desire as spirits of oneness is to experience physical life in a balanced partnership with the ego in this world of duality or opposites.

Being oneness and separation simultaneously.

The original human beings

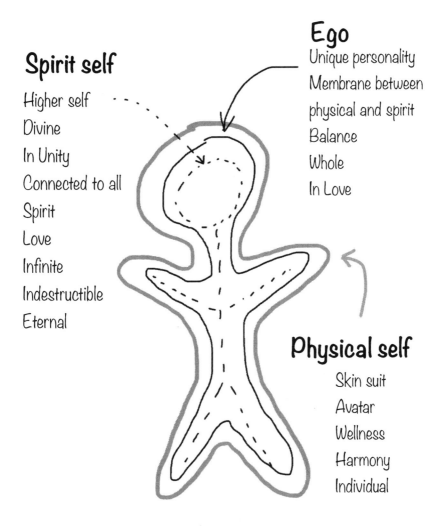

Spirit self

Higher self
Divine
In Unity
Connected to all
Spirit
Love
Infinite
Indestructible
Eternal

Ego

Unique personality
Membrane between
physical and spirit
Balance
Whole
In Love

Physical self

Skin suit
Avatar
Wellness
Harmony
Individual

Human being of Love

Ego bridge

Our ego tends to be portrayed as a mischievous scoundrel who needs to be mastered and controlled.

Here I present the ego as the vital bridging link between our spiritual and physical aspects. The glue that holds us together.

A vital part in our experience of enlightenment.

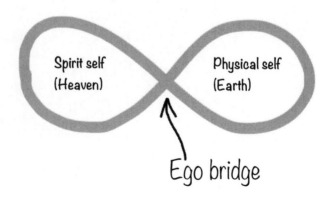

Spirit self
(Heaven)

Physical self
(Earth)

Ego bridge

Ego membrane

Our ego behaves as if it were a thin membrane, operating as a bridge between our spirit and physical selves. This is not a physical thing but a 'thought membrane', enabling the normally incompatible physical and spiritual domains to work together.

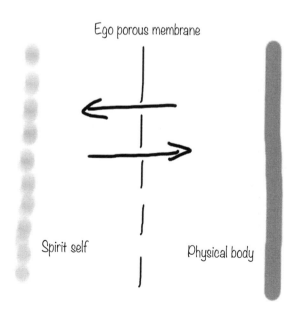

Ego porous membrane

Spirit self

Physical body

Unlocked

When in balance our mind can access both the physical and spiritual aspects of our lives. There is a flow and exchange of feelings across the ego membrane.
We can apply our creative individual identity to the collective unified whole and bring something new to the party.

From balance we can access enlightenment.

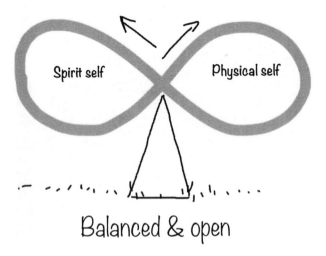

Spirit self   Physical self

Balanced & open

Balance

As a child we have no personality or ego as such, we carry with our spirit an identity and history from past lives that individualises us.

Then over our lifetime the ego personality develops and moves us into a place of balance.

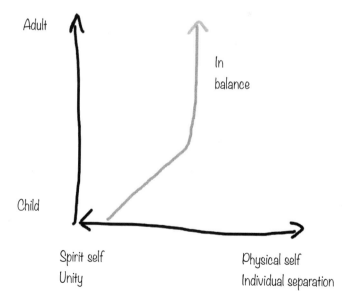

Adult

Child

In
balance

Spirit self
Unity

Physical self
Individual separation

Enlightenment

Once we are in a place of balance we can then choose to experience enlightenment which is the pinnacle of achievement in this physical environment because we become as an ascended master yet experience life here in the physical.

You no-longer need seek guidance outside, since you can access it all within.

Everything becomes transparent and open perceiving all other spirits as equal.

What is enlightenment?

Compassion

Harmony

Unselfish Love

Trust

Absolute Serenity

Total connection

Peace

Oneness

Divinity

The key to everything

Open to everyone

Freedom

Self-awareness

Knowing

Bliss

Unity

Acceptance

Selfless

Humility

Neutrality

Balance

And so much more....

Unselfish Love

The experience of enlightenment is beyond our intellectual capability, since it resides in a different place, that of feeling and Love.

The two most profound aspects of enlightenment are oneness with all and an experience of unselfish Love.

The two are actually inseparable, when you experience Unity you will immediately experience unselfish Love and vice versa.

They are actually the same.

This place has another name, the zero point.

Love lost

Way back in time, in the very beginning we existed as a creature of Love, balancing the spiritual and the physical worlds. Creating beauty in harmony with nature.

Things never remain the same, change is a fundamental activity within our flowing universe.

Fast forward to the present day and things are very different. Today we exist as creatures who have lost their harmonious connection to divine Love.

2
Love Lost

Enlightenment lost

A grim picture emerges

A word of warning, this chapter paints rather an unpleasant picture of spiritual life in our modern world. One that may conflict with your own understanding. Your mind is portrayed as the rascal who prevents you from making any real progress with the evolution of your consciousness.

It is necessary to understand why the development of your consciousness is difficult, because this highlights a short cut that we can exploit to give us direct access to our inner spirit self.

Why?

The temptation at this point is to shoot off at a tangent and try to explain why things are the way they are in the world.

It does not really matter why, this is an external distraction to our personal self-discovery.

If we accept things as the way they are in the world and focus our attention upon the one area of which we have greatest influence, namely our mind.

We will concentrate upon the personal changes that have happened within us from the perspective of our ego, since this is the key to growing our consciousness.

Identity crisis

We come into this body as a divine being, this is what we are conscious of and relate to as. We are both a part of the collective divine consciousness and also a soul consciousness. Our goal is to balance both these aspects with our ego identity.

As we develop and mature as humans, society nurtures the ego to move you out of balance, becoming conscious only of being a physical identity.

You are unaware of the divine consciousness and soul consciousness that is your spirit self.

I am physical

Your whole reality is now defined by your
physical and ego consciousness.

As far as your ego is concerned there is no
spiritual aspect to you, it behaves like a
hollow shell.

You 'think' you are only a physical body with
a conscious and unconscious mind.

This is an illusion.

Physical body

Ego

Spirit
self

Enlightenment?

Today very few people achieve an enlightened condition where you no-longer need seek guidance outside, since you can access it all within. Some humans claim to be enlightened, yet they seek guidance from other spirits.

The world conspires against your soul's ambition to achieve enlightenment.

Contrary to what you may have been told, enlightenment is within reach of every human being on the planet at this time.

It is our birth right.

Why aren't we enlightened?

Ignorance

Money

Ego

FEAR

Separation

Dis-unity

Beliefs

Time - too busy

Values

Religion

Society

Self-discipline

Obligations

Sabotage

Being number one

Our selves

Family commitments

Pressures

Expectations

Conditioning

Arrogance

Ignorance

Mind chatter

No freedom

Other agendas

No Love

And so much more....

How did we get into this crazy situation?

Planned limitation

It is of no co-incidence that we have just described the opposite to enlightenment. For hundreds of generations our lives have been nurtured to move us away from our natural human condition.

When we are enlightened, the activities of all other humans and spirit beings become transparent to us.

We are deliberately blocked from achieving all-knowing enlightenment by those people and beings who do not want their activities to be exposed.

History

The world in which we live today is very different to that presented by religions, the media and history books.

We live in a place where we are purposefully being kept from achieving a state of enlightenment. Every aspect of our western culture is geared towards these aims.

I explained this history in more detail from the perspective of Love in the first book of the Love series 'Love: Our Lost Story'. Here we will concentrate upon our mind and the role of the ego in all this.

Self-limiting

Your ego has been nurtured and developed over your lifetime to become self-limiting, through fears and a lack of understanding about who we truly are.

Your mind has been perfected to limit and restrict your evolution. Your ego is policing yourself. Our personalities develop addictive behaviours which restrict us and throw up endless barriers to block our progress.

Returning back to your natural human condition of enlightenment is almost impossible.

Ego barrier

Our once porous thin membrane, operating
as a bridge between our spirit and physical
selves becomes a barrier. Isolating our inner
spiritual self.

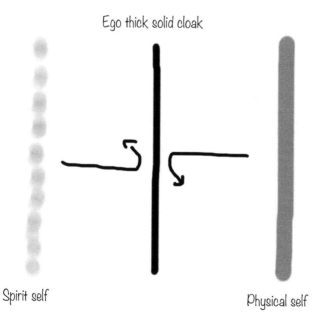

Ego thick solid cloak

Spirit self

Physical self

Ego mind cloak

If enlightenment can be described as experiencing oneness and unselfish Love, our egos have a strategy to block you from experiencing both.

Experiencing oneness is withheld from us by the ego bridge, the thin porous membrane hardens into a 'mind cloak' for separation, concealing our divine spirit self and the Love within. Our connection to Unity remains intact but unavailable to us during our daily lives.

The impenetrable ego mind cloak obstructs you from experiencing unselfish Love by using emotions and fears to push us into a condition of selfish individualism, looking after number one.

Bridge keeper

This separation means that your soul which is your source and the reason you are here, cannot communicate across the hardened cloak bridge with the physical you.

It is trapped inside and blocked from achieving your soul's desires in this life. However we still receive nudges from our spirit self in the form of deja-vu.

Human beings today

Ego

Cloaks and hides the spirit self

No spiritual connection

Out of balance

NO LOVE

FEAR

Spirit self

Separation

Difficult to hear

Love hidden

It remains divine, intact, infinite and indestructible connected to all except you!

Physical self

Illness

Ageing

Human being of No-Love

Holey cloaks

The ego cloak thickens over your lifetime, it comes from beliefs and habits. You own this cloak and have constructed it under the supervision of the society we live in.

This is a cloak of thoughts.

The cloak separates you from your divine aspect, you become disconnected from all and this results in individual selfish behaviour.

Our eyes provide small holes through the cloak and sometimes you get a glimpse of people's souls through their eyes.

The eyes are the window to the soul

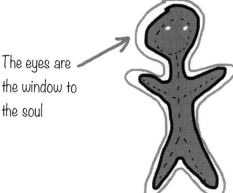

Separation

Separation

We experience separation from ourselves,
physical family, soul family and community.
Separation is the opposite of Unity,
becoming a direct block to enlightenment.

Our egos have been nurtured by society to
maintain you in a condition of total
separation. To isolate you from the oneness
that you share with everything.

There is little need for external control
because your ego as an adult is perfectly
developed to limit you and exploit your
personal weaknesses.

Separate self

The separate self is the identification with being number one in your life.

The ego will go to great efforts in nurturing your fears and weaknesses to keep you from venturing outside of the separate self into your spirit self and experiences of oneness. It will outmanoeuvre all your efforts.

Separateness brings envy, lust, jealousy, excitement, fear and desire and so on.

Fundamentally it only trusts information received by your physical senses. All information from the spiritual domain is distrusted.

"I will believe it if I see it", is the cry of the ego.

Lifetime

Our goal is to mature into a balanced human being with equal access to our spirit and physical selves. What actually transpires is that over our lifetime the ego personality dominates and smothers our spirit self and moves us completely out of balance.

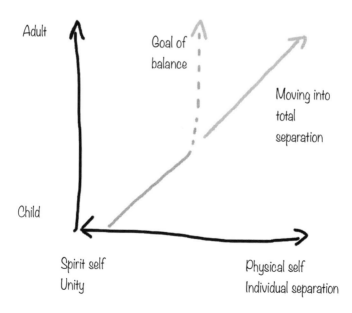

How we are limited

Separation and division by nations, states, towns, suburbs, skin colour, sexuality, politics, culture, religion, income and so on.

Our sensitivity is reduced by sweeteners, fluoride, Wi-Fi, cell phones, drugs and food additives, the list is endless.

Our mind is distracted by the internet, news, TV, money, work, artificial social time etc.

Technology has an added astral dimension which influences you and takes your energy, as do sacred geometry cities and the modification of our language.

The limitations are endless.....

Modern spirituality

Reviewing beliefs

If you participate in religious or 'new age' activities, then this chapter is for you.

Many people believe that the new age and modern church movements are the solution to our spiritual problems. I wish to challenge this belief and stimulate a re-thinking or re-programming. I am not asking you to agree with my views, but simply to take a deeper look at your spiritual activities and beliefs.

Most people are working from the goodness of their hearts, with love and compassion. I am not questioning the people, but the belief systems in which they work.

Religion

Religions promote a route to enlightenment that is open to all. They are well represented and tend to be easily accessible.

Their teachings are always based upon great fundamental truths which were first told by individuals who had a pure message. This core message resonates deeply within us.

However, over time the messages have been modified and manipulated, the outcome is that the route to enlightenment becomes almost impossible to complete. People reach some half way houses of bliss along the way and get no further.

New age religion

Just when you think that you have escaped
society's control and the rigid belief systems
of the churches and found freedom within
the spiritual new age movement you have
walked into a modern minefield.

It claims to free and empower you, but in
reality it restricts your growth. The common
pattern is of people flying high for a few
years and then they come crashing down. I
meet people who think that they have
achieved a higher consciousness, but there
is little evidence of them living in the
experience of unselfish Love and Unity.

Positivity

Modern spirituality imposes positivity, you can't express anger or disagree. Facebook is awash with fluffy spiritual messages with pretty pictures. People strive to become 'love and light'. Emotions considered negative are suppressed. Question this publicly and you are considered an evil threat.

This lack of negative expression is out of balance, life is not all love and light, it carries some tough emotional experiences, if these are not expressed and dealt with they are stored into our cellular memory, to be dealt with later and often manifest as emotional problems or diseases.

Technical spirituality

Our ego loves to learn and understand.

Western spirituality has become dominated by skilful teachers specialising in narrow fields. Each area is rationalised and explained in great detail.

The outcome is that we become engrossed in particular subject areas, all the time distracting ourselves from the basics of unselfish Love and Unity to be found within.

Outward facing

There is an obsession with asking questions and analysing. We are overwhelmed with complex systems of development.

The whole movement is outward facing and geared towards distracting you from the 'now', whatever its rhetoric.

Help and advice is pushed upon you from earthly and non-Earthly sources. People become reliant upon external sources of information. All this reinforces your belief that you are somehow limited in your personal capabilities.

Flattering the ego

Many of the modern approaches to spiritual growth do not threaten the separate selfish self. They flatter and strengthen the ego and encourage you to become involved in external distractions such as channelling, auras, psychic power and so forth and side-track you from your inner spirit self.

All forms of so called development will bring problems for you in the longer term if they are not coming from a place of unselfish Love and oneness.

Your spirit self will pull you back onto the right track whether you like it or not.

Light workers

In this world of duality, there is light and dark, good and bad. If you choose to work for the light and fight the dark, you are selecting a side, this moves you into a position where you cannot possibly experience unselfish Love.

As a being of the divine, you are neutral, neither light nor dark. By becoming involved in fighting for the 'light' this actually takes you further away from your true self.

People confuse love and light, light is simply the polar opposite to darkness, yet Love applies to everything. Love is light and dark and all the shades in-between.

Ancestors

Honour and respect your ancestors, they represent the great wave of evolution that carries you upon its crest.

But, putting too much attention into past lives becomes a distraction to the now moment.

Glance at the past but do not stare.

Heal the world

Many spiritual movements face outwards
with an emphasis upon healing other people
and the world. We are all encouraged to
become healers.

This is easier than healing yourself and does
not serve your own development. Yet
another distraction.

How can you reliably heal others when you
yourself require healing, what are you
passing on?

Healer heal thyself.

Road to nowhere

If you search for spiritual evolution you will never find it. It simply keeps moving away because your belief that it is difficult to access keeps pushing it away. Often you think you are closer, but this is your ego telling you that you are getting better at spirituality.

All the book reading and attending seminars satisfies your belief that you will find what you are looking for elsewhere. When in reality it is within.

Since birth you have been on a journey that takes you further away from the answer which is right here under your nose. This is the difference between knowing the path and walking the path.

Hang up your hat

Simply accept that everything is ok, that there is no rush.

Cease searching and give yourself space to re-connect to your core spirit self, it is here and has never been away. No training, rituals or special knowledge is required.

Take off all your explorers' paraphernalia and grab a comfy seat by the fire, warm your toes and relax. This is where the exploration of consciousness really happens.

Give yourself the space and you will re-discover your true self.

Ego
programming

Programming

The popular term used to describe the way
that we receive the standard beliefs and
values that we hold is cultural programming.

Standardised beliefs limit your creative
capability, they box you into a predictable
behaviour. Define how you think and act.

Programming takes many forms and there is
no escape from it, this book is influenced by
my personal programming.

The programmers

Others write our program, the beliefs they give you control your behaviour and define how you react emotionally to the world about you.

Accept that the programming is there, it is now a part of you. This is simply the way things are, if we try to fight the programming it will create stronger defences.

Observe your emotions, moments of high emotion are often a result of programming.

Observe, don't fight it.

Perfect separation

Although the condition of the planet and humanity may appear grim from our perspective, remember that we are here to experience Unity and in order to do this we must experience and understand separation.

Various forces acting on this planet have exploited mankind for their own needs. The side effect of this is that they have engineered a perfect separation, helping us move towards maximum stretch.

The pull from source is now so great that we will 'ping' back as a whole planetary consciousness as we reach maximum extension. In reading this, you are already feeling the pull of source.

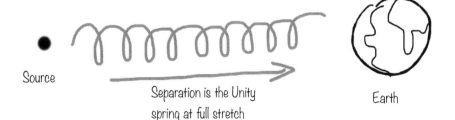

Source

Earth

Separation is the Unity spring at full stretch

No Entry

Our egos will block all our efforts at connecting with our spirit self. It is ruthless in the way that it bars our access.

Meditation may offer us short periods of relief, but unless you are highly adept you will be unable to maintain a meditative state whilst in full consciousness, during your daily life.

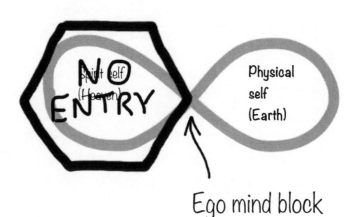

Ego mind block

Ego
addict

Addicted to pain

The ego behaves as an addict, in other words you have a tendency to act in ways that are bad for you and avoid things that are good for you. The ego is very difficult to overcome because it is perfectly tuned to your personality, it knows and exploits your every weaknesses.

The ego thrives from difficulty and striving, tough hard won progress, it's all 'no pain no gain'.

You go away for a weekend of blissful spiritual workshops, a few days later you are back to your old ways, in a place of fear.

The addict remains in control.

Addicted to the physical

Your addictive ego has been developed throughout your life by society and schooling. Our civilisation then presents you with endless addictive opportunities as products and services.

The modern world becomes a highly refined addict's playground.

All the people around you are physical world junkies and cannot comprehend why you should consider breaking the habit.

All of this distracts you from developing your consciousness.

Your ego will lie to you, prevaricate and keep you occupied with other activities.

Addicted to doing

The ego has no time for 'being' and will occupy all its time 'doing'. This is made increasingly difficult when all the people about you are busy doing stuff.

This doing keeps you from being happy long term, you receive short quick fixes which necessitate even more doing to get another fix, whether this is eating, shopping, drinking, competing, whatever your hang-up.

Many of these addictive pursuits tend to be individual in nature, further developing the sense of separation.

Addicted to Inaction

The ego prefers not to become involved, it will pay other intrepid explorers to discover and experience how to grow their consciousness and then learn intellectually from them.

The ego strategically avoids any spiritual experience because this may weaken the cloak.

We exchange our money for books and workshops, we are impressed, then we walk away and the ego does nothing.

This is another form of separation from our spirit self.

Addicted to delay

When we see opportunities for great change, a few brave ones become involved and immerse themselves in the experience, whilst the rest watch and wait, in the hope that things will get better.

The ego behaves like a bully, lacking in bravery, it plays safe avoiding new experiences and keeps its head down. It will stir things up and create drama but only when it is not threatened.

The ego allows you to dream about your hidden talent and look forward to your potential, but it is not for now.

Spirituality Anonymous

The first step when dealing with all addictions is to acknowledge that you have an addiction.

The next step is to make the choice, through your free will to change the situation.

This decision must be wholehearted and with conviction and desire otherwise you are wasting your time.

Spiritual
ego

Ego seeker

The spiritual seeker aspect of your ego
loves to learn techniques and methods, it
desires new abilities. It encourages new
activities where it can add another skill to its
portfolio. The ego approaches the whole
agenda from the perspective of power rather
than unselfish Love.

It rewards you after each spiritual book read
or course attended with thoughts that you
are becoming more spiritual.

It holds the promise of enlightenment at a
great distance from you and ensures that
you will not find it in this lifetime.

Spiritual Ego

Intellectual spirituality is the way of the ego,

* Gets the point
* Understands our divinity
* Thinks loving positive thoughts
* Comprehends what it is to be humble
* Grasps the idea of Unity
* Identifies with unselfish Love
* Makes sense of enlightenment

But does not feel it.

Ego's slow path

There are two approaches to development.

1/ Open route; this is fast and flowing, it involves listening and observing, learning from everyone about you. Listening to your inner guidance and simply being in peace and harmony. Experiencing unselfish Love. All totally boring for the ego.

2/ Closed route; this has much drama, this is the school of hard knocks, slow and difficult, only listening to guru teachers, an emotional roller coaster. No pain no gain. Life becomes a test. Emotions intensify as you try harder to connect to your spirit self.

Who could possibly want to travel down the open route when you can have great excitement with the closed route?

Ego relationships

We live our lives through our egos, this means that all our relationships are between egos, even our loving relationships have little engagement with our spirit self.

From the perspective of Love, our relationships invariably are selfish love, where there is give and take, a demand for attention, jealousy and a need to control the other person.

You are satisfying your ego and the ego of the other person.

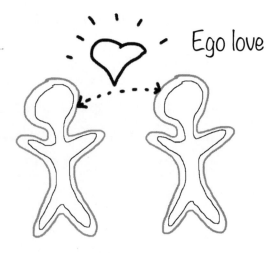

Ego love

Ego
mastery

The spiritual journey

Spiritual teachings are directed towards mastering 'weaknesses' this requires tremendous discipline to overcome the ego gently.

Progress is tough with the ego creating barrier after barrier, it is relentless and endless. We are told that it is good for us, all part of the human experience!

Some people wear their traumas as badges of spiritual honour.

It is almost hopeless.

Sneaking past the ego

Because the ego is drawn to drama and relishes being attacked. A common approach takes advantage of this by making changes discreetly and gently, so as not to arouse the suspicions of the ego.

It requires great self-discipline, strong will power, concentration and persistence to slowly and regularly work to control the mind, gradually increasing the length of the activities such as meditation until they become the greater part of your life.

Unfortunately this is generally incompatible with life in the world that we have, the ego will fight back too?

Break the ego

You can take the slow, hard ego friendly route or choose the tough fast track approach.

The ego hates the fast track because it will end in total destruction of the ego. It will endeavour to talk you out of it.

Go cold turkey and spend thirty days and thirty nights in the desert fasting.

Throughout history all the great spiritual leaders have taken this course.

This is a dangerous route too, if you are spiritually inexperienced it can throw you completely out of spiritual and physical balance.

The ego as your enemy

There is a fundamental flaw with our contemporary spiritual teachings, which focus upon mastering and breaking the ego.

If you put your attention into something then you simply give it your energy. If you spend your lifetimes spiritual journey in a quest to overcome your egos unwanted behaviours you make it stronger. You are locked into an arms race with your own mind. As you adopt new approaches to still the mind, the ego fights back with counter measures.

Your ego actually uses your spirituality for control, it is always seeking external answers to distract you.

You are at war with yourself, chasing your own tail. With your death comes no real progress, you are back where you started.

The ego as your friend

Rather than treating your ego as a villain or demon and giving it all your energy, I propose an alternative approach where we cease fighting with the ego and simply let it be.

A change of perspective permits us to look upon our egos as an untapped resource and enables us to transform it into our greatest asset.

3
Recovering
Love

Alternative path

Ambitious

We are commonly advised to focus our efforts upon the 'next small step' of the journey. This is simply limiting ourselves into believing that we can only make one small step at a time.

This constrained belief manifests this way, it becomes your reality and you are restricted into making small steps. You become self-limiting.

If however we focus upon achieving the highest spiritual condition available to humanity, then this becomes achievable within our lifetime.

How close is enlightenment?

Question: What is the difference between an unbalanced being of no-love and fear and a harmonious being of Love and Unity?

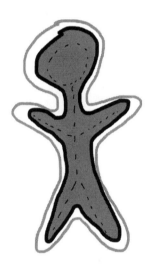

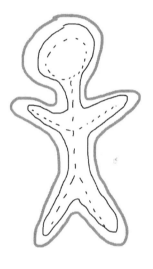

Today; a being of separation and fear

Our goal; an enlightened being of Love

Answer: It's all in the mind, you are simply a thought away. So near yet so far.

The gurus say it's easy

Listen to the top billing teachers and they are all instructing us how to achieve a higher consciousness, by simply changing the way that you think. Most of the teachers are unique in that they have a level of mind mastery that is alien to the rest of us.

We all understand this, we know that we need to spend more time in meditation, think more positively and calm our minds. Move from emotions into feelings and so on. It's a no brainer.

Yet we are unable to do this, we are being blocked. Not by the world outside, but by our own mind.

There must be another way

If a gigantic mountain blocks your way, do you blindly climb up it or do you look for alternatives.

This raises a few basic questions;
Do we have to tackle our ego head on?
Can we work on our strengths rather than weaknesses?
Are all the teachings really working in our favour?

For a moment let us ignore all the traditional complex spiritual teachings, and dream up a simple easy approach that is accessible to everyone and requires no discipline or special knowledge.

Our assets

Auditing our strengths

Most spiritual development approaches work on the basis of overcoming weaknesses and confronting our all-powerful ego. Since we have an addictive ego there is only a slim chance of success.

Following extensive research, modern business management favours the development of staff strengths rather than the more traditional approaches where staff weaknesses were developed. The spiritual community have not yet caught on, they are still using old traditional methods.

Let's begin by looking at a few of our unique strengths that we all share as humans.

Re-programmable

The idea is simple, whatever you have been programmed with by society can simply be re-programmed by ourselves. Our brains are wonderfully versatile and can be re-programmed many times.

Changing your beliefs is a form of re-programming. This is very tricky when the ego is working against you, but simple when it's on your side.

Born to act

We are excellent actors, wearing many masks in our daily life. Carl Jung and others have described the different archetypes that we 'play' during our lives.

Acting is something that we can do without even having to think about it.

This is a highly complex activity, a skill we all possess, doing a little real acting in our lives should come quite easily.

Heart of the matter

One of our greatest dormant assets is the heart energy centre located in the middle of our chest.

We associate the heart with Love.

The heart is at the centre of our lives and offers a direct link to our spirit self, to our soul.

Once activated our heart offers a sensitive sixth sense.

The heart also radiates out your feelings to the world, broadcasting who you are.

May the force be with you

There is a wise old proverb that says 'where your mind's attention goes, your power follows it '.

Another way of saying this is that we can consciously direct our energy.

If we were to focus our attention upon our heart centre, then we would power our spiritual identity and our Love.

Ego neutralised

There is a beneficial side effect to this shift in attention to the heart. By diverting our attention away from the chattering mind, with its thoughts about the past and future we take power away from our ego.

The ego bully is predictable, bullies crave attention. They do this by provoking you into reacting either by fighting back or running away.

If you ignore bullies they eventually get bored and ignore you.

An ego ignored is an ego neutralised.

From disorder comes order

There are well documented accounts of patients diagnosed with multiple personality disorders experiencing a physical illness in one personality and good health in an alternate personality.

This demonstrate that the human psyche can carry multiple personalities with complete physical independence.

Could we create a new personality that our ego would be unaware of?

Yes we can.

Attraction does the work

The law of attraction is driven from your
heart feeling, if we work from this space we
are empowering ourselves to change our life
without effort.

You attract not what you want with your
mind but attract what you are feeling within
your heart right now.

Feeling

The ego operates from thinking and with emotions.

If we adopt the use of feelings rather than thinking we have another approach where we can by-pass our ego.

Fortunately the heart centre is also the centre of our ability to experience feelings.

We are in great shape to unlock our ego and balance our spiritual and physical existence, we have all the assets we need.

Next we look at how we can put all these ideas together and take control of our lives.

How?

A cunning plan

By pulling all our assets together, we could....

Act from the heart and with feeling a new personality that portrays your divine spirit self.

The newly acted character would be independent from your ego and they would co-exist in harmony.

After a while the acted character becomes the foundation of your current personality.

You simply become your true self, in balance with the ego. We can then explore Unity and unselfish Love.

Effortless.

Serene self

I call my personal divine character my Serene Self, please feel free to personalise yours.

This character represents our enlightened spirit self and has all the virtues of enlightenment that were listed earlier.

Next we look at how we can make this character come alive.

If you are already an experienced thespian then you can probably skip the next chapter.

Spiritual
acting
school

Acting

We will now take a short course on acting to bring our 'serene self' character to life.

The typical stages of acting are:
1/ Describe the character
2/ Learn how to feel the character and own it
3/ Rehearse in a safe environment
4/ Perform on stage (the real world)

Please don't take this too seriously, it is supposed to be fun.

Method acting

A tried and tested approach to bringing a character alive is called Method Acting. This technique requires the actor to act the part with feeling which is ideal for our role. It also makes use of personal experiences, and builds the new character upon these. The feeling of the character becomes totally personal and unique to you.

We will borrow a couple of techniques from method acting.

Serene self character

Some facets of the character are;
- Compassionate
- In Harmony, balanced
- Experiences Unselfish Love
- Trusting
- Absolute Serenity and peace
- Total connection with all, in unity
- Self aware
- Inner Knowing
- Blissful
- Accepting
- Humble
- Neutral

List all the individual aspects of your divine spirit self, using your own words.

Owning the serene self

The crucial point is to do this through feelings and emotions that you have experienced in your life, applying them to the individual character traits of the serene self.

This has the advantage that you are not creating something new but simply using what you already have as a unique individual. A collection of bespoke experiences.

Against a few of the aspects find experiences from your life where you felt that way.

For example,
Unity.........a moment in nature when ......
Love.........a feeling shared with...

Character collage

Create a collage of images that particularly
resonate with your new character. Ideally
with some photos from your own life. Select
images that stimulate particular feelings that
relate to the virtues of your divine character.

If you come across any images that bring
back unpleasant memories then save these
and we will revisit them later.

Magic if

What if I were......my serene self? This gives you permission to believe that you are something different, that you are not currently experiencing. This comes completely naturally to children.

Play at being a child again, acting out various roles, without awkward or self-conscious feelings.

Enter into particular parts of the character and experience again those original feelings triggered by memories or the collage.

If you can't find any suitable memories or images, simply imagine what it would be like.

Act Divine

Bring some of the different aspects
together, cherry picking the ones that work
best for you. Recall the feelings that you
listed earlier and re-live them.

See the world through the eyes of your
divine higher self. Become neutral, free of
opinions and emotions. Slow down.

Ask the question, how would my serene self
feel about this? Then experience the feeling.

Being divine.

Physical sensations

As you act the role more often, you may begin to notice some physical changes that emerge the moment you step into the role. Simply observe what happens.

It could be a slow deep intake of breath, a yawn, loosening of the shoulders, pace of walking slows, slowing the speed at which you eat, a clearing of the mind, any number of different things.

Some of these are outcomes that you would normally have to concentrate on to achieve.

When acting your serene self, they come for free, without effort.

Acting from your heart

Moving deeper

Now that we have a feel for what your personalised serene self role will feel like, we will begin to engage our heart centre.

The heart acts both as a receiver, a sixth sense of the world about you and also as a transmitter.

You are broadcasting your heartfelt emotions, not what you think but how you feel. It shares your true feelings.

You are also broadcasting who you are, your soul identity. This explains why you are attracted to certain people.

Heart centre

Our heart centre in the middle of our chest level with our physical heart is the central point of our energy the core of our essence. The middle energy chakra as described in Indian energy wisdom. Love is associated with the heart.

When we gesture 'I am' we place our hand in the middle of our chest.

Our language still contains many references to the importance of the heart;
 - The heart of the matter
 - Straight from the heart
 - With all my heart
 - Follow your heart
 - Heart's desire and so on....

Open heart

Many methods are available to open up your heart energy centre such as yoga fire breath. I won't go into detail here because, this is already covered by many excellent authors.

For simplicity you can visualise with your in-breath drawing energy up through your feet and down through your crown into your heart centre, and with the out-breath feeling your heart open, as Love pours out of your body, filling you and the room with Love.

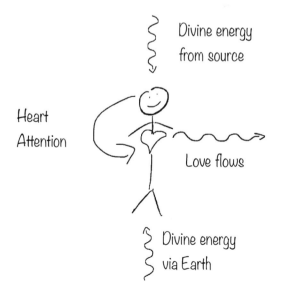

Divine energy
from source

Heart
Attention

Love flows

Divine energy
via Earth

Opening your heart

You can use various techniques to further
open your heart, a very simple approach is
to use anything that touches you deeply and
gives you that loving feeling such as art,
music, movies, children, people, pets etc.

Whilst in the loving place bring your attention
to your heart centre.

Sometimes we have to put a little effort into
opening up our hearts, but once opened it
will look after its self, provided that you
make a habit of putting your attention into
your heart space.

Heart attention

Direct your power to your heart, by keeping your attention upon your heart centre.

Begin by placing a finger in the centre of your chest, become aware of the pressure. Remove your finger and maintain your attention upon that spot.

Your attention upon the heart centre energises your heart. It melts the thick ego cloak which conceals your spirit self and restores your connection to soul.

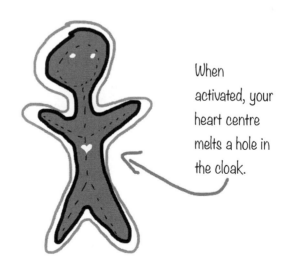

When activated, your heart centre melts a hole in the cloak.

Heartfelt acting

Experience your serene self with your
attention upon your heart centre.

Acting not half-hearted but whole-heartedly,
experience the serene self feelings again,
but this time whilst you maintain your
attention upon your heart centre.

Does it feel different? Observe the changes
in your perspective.

Serene switch

When you begin to act from heartfelt feeling,
be clear in your mind that you are entering
your serene self.

Your mind will learn this and after a little
practice, you only need to think the words
'serene self' and you will automatically
switch over to the feeling.

This is child's play, there is no need to make
it complicated.

Serene eyes

When you visit unfamiliar places, you observe much more and see great detail in small things.

You also become aware of the 'feeling' of the new place, this is an experience you rarely have during your day to day life. We lose sensitivity when in familiar places.

When our minds are in a new environment they turn up the sensitivity, looking for potential dangers.

Observe the change in sensitivity when you act your serene self, familiar places become fresh to you, there is detail that you never noticed before.

Explore your divine role

Conscious rehearsals

Practice experiencing your serene self in a safe environment, if possible out in nature or in a beautiful place.

When you rehearse keep your eyes open, this is not meditation where you disconnect from the world, we want to experience and feel it. Consciousness is the key to the serene experience, it is also more potent if you avoid stimulants, drugs and alcohol.

By being in a fully conscious state, aware of the world about us, it helps us experience our connection to everything, the core aspect of enlightenment, Unity.

Rehearsals for fun

When you act your serene self with heart feeling, your sensitivity to blissful experiences take you to a whole new level. It's like a super sense.

Enter into your serene self and experience food, music, movies, hugs and nature. It amplifies positive experiences.

Ego soaps

Your ego loves to act out soap opera dramas with your mind. The dramas are short, very, very repetitive, have little interesting content and lack creativity.

The soaps are usually based around historical events from your life that stirred strong emotions at the time.

The ego over plays the moments of drama and dramatises the emotions from the moment they were recorded.

Events tend to be dramatised in a way that does not accurately reflect the reality of the incident.

Top billing soaps

Spend some time compiling a list of the most annoying repetitive soaps that are played out in your mind, day in day out. These are your ego's top billing mind dramas.

You know the scripts off by heart, a bonus of repeats!

Taking one drama at a time, we are going to create an ending by watching the drama from the objective perspective of our serene self. Allowing the serene self to observe the drama from neutrality and put a truthful perspective upon it.

Mind theatres
Present

Ego's most

popular

SOAPS

Axing the soaps

If the scene involves other people observe them from the serene self, don't rationalise or think too much, just observe how it feels. Observe the other actors as aspects of your personality, how does this make you feel?

Experience the drama from their perspective and ask.
Why do they behave this way?
What are their vulnerabilities?

Write down your feelings, express them in whatever way feels right. This neutralises the drama and brings the scene to an end.

Mind theatres
Present
Ego's
Last
Episode

Emotional Images

Earlier we created a collage of images and put some images to one side that provoked emotions that we would call negative. These could include images of people in our lives with whom we have had unpleasant relationships with.

Repeat the earlier exercise with the soaps, taking one image at a time and processing the emotions into feelings and then a release. This is not something to rush, you could spend days with some images.

Acting in real life

Private acting

The serene self is of unselfish Love and is humble, share your serene self experiences only where appropriate.

When acting your serene self, no one will be aware of what you are doing, they don't need to be, although some may feel the change in you.

This is internal to you, a privately acted performance. At this stage in your acting career the experience is for you alone.

Real life scenes

You have experimented with your serene self playing 'recorded' dramas, now it is time to explore life's 'live' dramas.

Begin by entering your serene self at random safe moments during the day, whilst doing the regular activities of life, working, eating, travelling, washing and so on.

Simply observe if you feel differently, for example does it change your feeling towards the food you eat.

Difficult emotions

Powerful emotions are the first sign that the ego is creating a dramatic scene.

Watch your emotions and the moment you become aware that an emotion is about to kick off, move into your serene self.

Observe from the perspective of your serene self, the scene unfolding before you, behave how you would normally behave and feel how your serene self would do it differently.

Allow your serene self to show you an alternative interpretation of the scene.

The serene self processes emotions rather than keeping them hidden and stored, go with the flow, do what you feel is needed to clear the unwanted emotions.

Re-experience

The serene self opens the doors wide to try
again all those spiritual techniques that
never quite succeeded before, when they
were derailed by the ego.

Revisit all the techniques that resonated
with you before, such as affirmation and
visualisation, this time practice them whilst
acting your serene self.

Observe the difference.

Relationships

We can now revisit our personal relationships from the perspective of the serene self.

Look afresh at all the attachments to people and things, what do these now mean to you? Losing your selfish attachment does not mean breaking all your links, it is simply a change in perception.

Find new friends who are on an unselfish path, they will invariably be attracted to you.

Unselfish Love is about feeling the same way towards a stranger as a close friend.

Intermission

Pause for reflection

What have we actually achieved by acting a new divine character?

Through this character you are experiencing brief moments of what it is to be your true self.

You have achieved the simple change to the way you think that all the gurus are encouraging you to do.

You are beginning to experience your truth and the acted character will slowly morph into your true self, it will become you.

Being truth.

Natural faith

Begin by accepting the feasibility of the 'idea' of oneness and unselfish Love.

Believe not in what you hear or read from others. (Including this book)

Have true faith only when you know from direct experience.

You have the gift now.

Are you waiting for something? The next life perhaps!

Enlightenment revisited

Now that we have a way to experience a more balanced relationship between our ego and divine spirit self we can freely explore enlightenment without being derailed by our ego.

The two fundamental aspects of enlightenment are being in Unity with everything and being in unselfish love. The two go hand in hand.

We shall begin with Unity because this is more accessible.

Illusion of separation

Free will is actually a concept that is derived from the idea of separateness, free will is about the individual.

We talk about a free will universe as if it were a special law imposed upon us, but it is inherent in oneness, free will is an expression of being in unity, it is simply how it is.

When you experience oneness, there is no longer any need for the notion of free will, because there is no separation. Separation is simply an illusion generated by your ego.

We move from the individual notion of free will into feeling the collective will, which is the desire of the whole collective.

4
Unity

Experience
Unity

Paradox

The greatest paradox is that you can only discover the existence of Unity by first being an individual experiencing separation.

We have successfully completed the experience of separation, we are now fully qualified to experience Unity.

Nothing else is required.

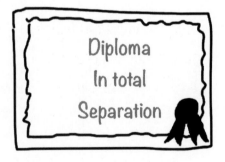

Diploma
In total
Separation

Feel Unity

Become aware of the feeling of yourself and
then extend that feeling outwards, illuminate
the world about you with your heart and feel
what you get back.

If you get the chance, go swimming in the
sea, experience the rain, or strong winds.
Feel it with your serene self.

We humans are life forces moving about in
an Earthly 'sea' of life force. This ocean
experiences oneness.

The connection between all things is
experienced through the process of
conscious giving and receiving.

It's all experience

The Universe is continuously evolving and changing, the underlying process responsible for this is giving and receiving which is a natural activity. Science describes it as a flow of energy. In reality this is a communication between two beings, an opportunity for experience and growth.

Nature uses a process of 'desire to receive for the sake of sharing'. This expands the act of giving. Creating more than that which was originally given. A plant creates more than the sunlight, air and soil gifted to it.

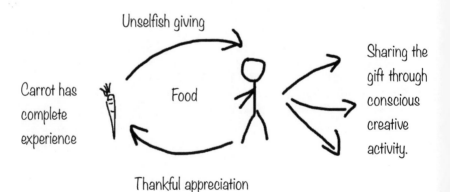

Unselfish giving

Carrot has complete experience

Food

Sharing the gift through conscious creative activity.

Thankful appreciation

Receiving

Modern day receiving

In our culture we close the cycle of giving and receiving with an exchange of money or goods. It's about give and take, a closed transaction. New age spirituality uses money as an 'energy exchange' in return for services.

We become indoctrinated into the 'ethical' behaviour of always reciprocating when we receive a gift. Receiving charity with no payback is frowned upon.

This limits the potential for experience and creation in each and every giving, there is a clear ending with no room for expansion.

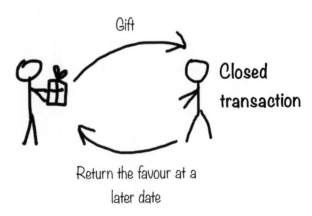

Gift

Closed transaction

Return the favour at a later date

Conscious receiving

Being conscious that we are receiving something gifted to us, assists the other beings to complete their experience of giving.

For example when eating a meal, consciously deconstruct the dish back to its component plants and animals, giving thanks to them. This is easy with home-made meals but difficult with processed food because you don't know what the components parts are.

Honour natures giving, the heat from the Sun or the scent of a flower, by honouring you fulfil the flowers and Suns experience.

Giving

Unconditional giving

The nature of the natural world is to give unconditionally, to bestow upon us. Humans test this by fighting, controlling and forcing nature. Even after our great onslaught, nature continues to give unconditionally.

We are nature and we share this as our natural way too.

Unconditionally give of your Love, this is an infinite resource within.

Harmonious giving

If you give, but deep down begrudge that you are having to do this then you are not in harmony, this can weaken you.

Giving from the ego tends to be selfish, it is usually looking for a pay back.

To ensure that you are in harmony, move into your serene self before you give, in this way you will be harmonious and you may be pleasantly surprised at how you feel.

True giving does not need thanks, it is unselfish.

Giving Love

This is not the same as giving away all your energy which is an integral part of what you are, if you give all your energy away you will destroy yourself.

Give from your inner infinite Love.

Give not of yourself but of your spirit.

I begin each day by sharing my Love unconditionally.

Daily Love share

There is a shamanic ritual 'calling in the directions' that is used for various purposes, fundamentally it is a simple way to address all spirit, this includes nature spirits, souls, non-Earthly spirits, everything.

I have modified the traditional call, to share my Love with all spirit. This is completely unconditional, I ask for nothing in return.

Each morning I carry out the share as a way of announcing my presence. The feelings I get back in response remind me about my connection to everything.

I am not a fan of rituals, most of which have an unclear meaning. This however is unambiguous, begin vocalising the words in order to understand the feelings. Later simply share your Love from feeling alone.

Unconditional Love share

Begin from the serene self, with a pure heart. Place soft attention upon the heart centre, visualising Love pouring out from the whole body.

Facing East:

"I share my infinite Love with the spirits of the East".

Facing South:

"I share my infinite Love with the spirits of the South".

Facing West:

"I share my infinite Love with the spirits of the West".

Facing North:

"I share my infinite Love with the spirits of the North".

Looking up:

"I share my infinite Love with the source of all".

Looking down:

"I share my infinite Love with Mother Earth".

Eyes closed, with a hand on the heart centre:

"I share my infinite Love with the deep mystery within me".

Experience the other

To complete the whole cycle of giving and receiving, we guide our attention to all those involved, drawing the whole activity into oneness. We begin by doing this with our imagination, later as we become more experienced we can focus upon feeling the whole activity.

Use your imagination to experience how the other being is experiencing what you give, for example if you stroke your cat, imagine how the cat feels. If you receive a freshly baked cake from a friend, imagine how they feel when they see how happy you are with this lovely gift.

Receiving
to share

Receiving and sharing

We can take an earlier example a step further, when receiving from nature when eating a meal, deconstruct the dish back to its component plants, give thanks to them and reflect on how you can share their gift. For example my last meal helped me write this, which I share with you. This helps you become conscious of your connections to nature.

When receiving to fulfil the needs of another, then our receiving becomes a form of giving and we form an energetic loop of experience between us.

Human sharing

Receiving to share creates the balance between giving and receiving. It makes the whole cycle work fully, maximising the experiences for all involved.

We humans can make an additional contribution by adding our individual creative talent through the power of our ego. We can creatively amplify the sharing.

For example if we collect some of the seeds from a plant we can then sow them in places that may have been inaccessible to the original plant.

Be creative and harmonious in your sharing.

Share your infinite inner Love.

Creators

Local creation

We manifest the world about us through attraction. The feeling deep within our heart has a vibration, our heart acts as a powerful transmitter, broadcasting your deep heartfelt feeling. These are like ripples from a stone thrown into a pond these ripple flow outwards and attract similar vibrations to you.

We attract or pull into our life people, animals, events and things that vibrate in the same way to us. We create the immediate local reality about us.

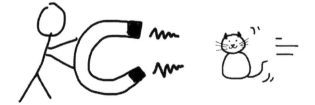

Global creation

Each person is creating ripples in the big pond of life, your vibration of attraction becomes diluted as you move further away from your heart.

As vibrations merge new vibrations unfold which represent your family, neighbourhood, town, country and the Earth.

The further we move away from our hearts our personal creative influence diminishes.

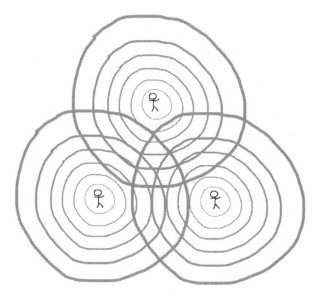

Everything is you

Because the world unfolds around you as a result of attraction, you have personally contributed to all that surrounds you in your close vicinity.

Look about you now, this is all a part of you and is another way of viewing Unity.

When you become aware that the world adjacent to you has actually been created by you, it immediately changes your relationship. The world becomes more intimate and has a direct connection to the feelings in your heart.

Your physical senses are perceiving the past that you created a moment ago.

5

Unselfish
Love

Love

Love is...

When we live from the ego, our experiences of human love tend to be selfish emotional love which is completely different in feeling from the divine Love within.

Divine Love is also different from the 'love' of beings of light, which tends to be dramatic and bright, very showy, full of glory and splendour, external to you, of one polarity, that of light. You become the amazed observer.

Divine Love is neutral, calm, feels like home, comfortable, no fanfares, no pomp and glory, it is deeply personal, beautiful and natural and you feel it both within and outside of you. It isn't dark or blindingly bright, almost understated. It simply is. You are involved, it is a part of you.

Love others

When you begin to live in your serene self,
the ego cloak which smothered your spirit
self begins to slip and you experience divine
Love with increasing regularity.

What was once inaccessible becomes
available to you.

Before working upon self Love, which has
been brutally programmed out of us,
experience giving Love to others from your
serene self.

Become familiar with this feeling. Observe
any emotions that come up, what physical
feelings do they generate? Bring these
feelings to the surface, deal with them
without over analysis.

Self Love

Healthy self Love

When we cease to 'think' of ourselves as having limited and flawed personalities and also remember that we are transcendent beings, self Love simply happens.

By cultivating our connection, feelings and awareness, rather than developing abilities we simply slip into this way of feeling.

To change our inner aspect, changes the thought programming that has taken place over our lifetime.

The ultimate outcome from self Love is good physical health as your body begins to reflect the Love that you carry within.

Self Love

For most people self is possibly the most
difficult of all the spiritual activities. Our ego
has been exceptionally successful at
blocking this experience.

Self Love comes naturally after loving others
first. If you self Love first, loving others does
not always follow unless you are very
securely in your serene self.

As you Love others, the Love flows freely
through you and this becomes another form
of self Love.

Express your self Love

Prepare for this carefully, make time in your life, this is very special and deserves the space not to be rushed.

Enter into your serene self fully, then stand in front of a mirror and visualise and feel an outflowing of Love from your spirit self to the awesome being in front of you. Observe your emotions and let them flow freely, you are releasing your natural Love which has been captive for such a long time.

Avoid becoming drawn into the drama of your emotions, simply observe them passively, from the perspective of your divine self, let them wash through, cry freely.

Unselfish Love

Unselfish Love

There are many facets of unselfish Love,
such as kindness, compassion,
harmlessness, humility and respect.

From your serene self meditate upon the
above words, what do they feel like? Their
meaning changes when viewed from your
divine perspective.

Patience

The key qualities of unselfish Love are patience and humility.

Patience is active waiting, not idleness.

In nature, plants may patiently wait for the rains.

Waiting is a state of being.

Making time and space for an understanding to unfold.

Humility

Humility is the opposite of being self-centred.

In harmony with the universe.

Surrendering to the divine within.

Accepting criticism, you do not have to 'appear' right.

Not seeking attention or credit from others.

Flowing with life.

Unconditional Love

There is no need to try, once in your serene self this experience is natural. When you experience Unity, this is also how you feel. The two go hand in hand.

See and feel how amazing you and everything is from this new perspective.

You now have access to the divine within you.

Experience how it feels, it is the beauty and compassion within.

Love of the child

Visualise your inner child, if a child's ego has not yet been programmed by family and society it will embrace its spirit self and express it with inner Love. What did you do when you were alone as a child?

- Daydream
- Marvel at nature
- Watch the clouds
- Observe and see the detail in everything
- Smile

Compassion

When you feel in oneness with everything,
you naturally feel and care for all beings
because they are you.

You no longer discriminate between eating
particular plants or animals, since all are
equal.

Compassionate giving is not blindly feeding
peoples wants and desires, it is giving what
their 'being' requires. This is giving with
Loving discretion.

If you have any concerns about becoming
selfish during giving, then give anonymously.
This is totally selfless.

6

True Self

What happens?

The more often you act your divine self from your heart centre, various side effects occur, you;

* Move away from being emotional.
* Become less reactive.
* Find your fears dissolving.
* Experience a sense of calm.
* Discover your intuition.
* Quietly observe the world unfolding.
* Observe changes within your family.
* Form a new relationship with food.

Eventually the serene self begins to kick in without you prompting it, often when you really need it.

You become true

Actors occasionally suffer from the problem where they become the acted role in their regular life. This is precisely the outcome that we desire.

Because the serene self is now tuned to your experiences, you simply become your true self without any effort.

You can give up the acting job, because you have discovered yourself.

Congratulations.

Losing your baggage

The ego carries a lot of emotional baggage. If we allow the serene self to take over our life, then all your fears, emotions, anxieties, pains and other undesirable emotions that belong to your ego, become a thing of the past. You are aware of them but they do not dominate your life.

One by one you can allow them to surface in your mind, where your serene self acting as an observer can process them.

Universal mind

Undeveloped egos tend to behave in a reactive, fearful and aggressive way, as the ego grows and recognises the divine spark for what it is, it begins to understand that it is not alone.

The whole behaviour of the ego changes and the cloak dissolves, the ego engages with Unity that is the universal consciousness.

Our goal is to harmonise all the different layers of our self and allow them to flow between themselves without boundaries. The ego self, higher self and divine self.

You can only access this change from a place of unselfish Love.

I Am

When you become your acted serene self,
you enter into a deep relationship with your
being, you become the 'I am presence'.

We are the abundance, we are all things
because we have been many things in past
lives.

Awesome.

Surrender

We are taught to surrender, to let go. It infers that we are somehow giving ourselves away. Some deities ask for us for total surrender to them, this is total disempowerment, it takes us completely out of balance, away from our natural condition.

An alternative safer way to view surrender is as an internal surrender, the ego surrenders to the inner spirit self.

Surrender to yourself.

You are all

It can all sound very grand and irrelevant to us when our minds are in a state of separation, but as you move into Unity the following words make more sense.

* You are everything.
* You cannot experience an identity crisis when you are everything.
* Prophesy is irrelevant when you are creating.
* You are the living essence of yourself, if you deny one aspect, you are lost. All is who you are.
* Feel and experience all life's experiences, positive negative and neutral, accept them all, these are experiences that you have created.
* If you feel anger but reject it, you are not expressing who you are, express it in an appropriate way.

When you are in separation you are actually trying NOT to be who you are!

Knowing

When you unlock your spirit self, your intuition comes alive. This is not an inner voice which comes from another being, but a knowing. You simply understand without having to 'hear' the information because it is already there.

When you know things that you were previously unaware of, this is you connecting direct to source without a being in the middle, human or otherwise adding its interpretation and views.

As knowing thoughts come to you, note them in a journal. If you have questions, ask them one at a time whilst experiencing the serene self.

Ego amigo

By creating an alternative character we have left our ego intact, we have not broken it down and defeated it as we would an enemy.

This means that our ego is still strong, leaving our individual unique personality whole and vibrant. Your ego becomes your friend and companion. You have a firm trusting foundation on which to build.

This is the point of balance where we maximise the benefits of our internal inner connection to the Unity of the divine, and our ego brings its individual unique creativity.

You are now in an optimum balanced position, spiritually and physically, to grow and explore your experiences.

Distractions

As you develop your awareness, you begin to see, hear and experience energy. Many people become drawn into energy phenomena and they become a distraction from their focus within.

Energy phenomena, hold no importance for your development, they are merely a by-product of the process of change.

Other spirits may compete for your attention and offer their wisdom. These too are a distraction.

Observe all phenomena, if they generate unwanted emotions, process them in the same way as we discussed earlier.

Physical changes

As the energies begin to flow through you, they can result in humming sensations, minor heart fluctuations, fuzzy vision, changes in breathing, spontaneous tears, involuntary smiling and so on.

This is energy flowing and energy can be steered with your awareness, most easily using your breath as a way to transport the energy through your body.

Visualise the energy being carried down through your body into the ground with each breath.

If you are unsure or uncomfortable with any changes, it is wise to seek help and advice. Follow your intuition.

Is this a Quick fix?

We are often reminded that there are no short cuts to our consciousness development. Much of this comes from people's personal experiences of a long and testing journey. Very much like human snakes and ladders, with numerous small steps up and the occasional backwards fall.

Religions and the whole spiritual industry have a lot invested into the message that this is difficult. Believe that it is difficult and it will manifest this way.

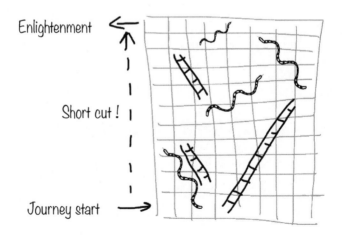

Commitment

In sharing this approach, I must be clear that it does not work without personal wholehearted commitment, if you fall back into the ego's old ways of thinking that it is beyond your abilities then the ego has regained control. When you become aware of the fears and insecurities kicking in, it is time to act your serene self again.

Now that you are no longer fighting your own ego, the effort required is minimal.

Experience enhancement

Once you have moved from occasional connections to your serene self, to being in this state for much of your day, you are well placed to get enhanced experiences from spiritual books and workshops.

Follow your inner guidance and select courses that resonate with your serene self. Consciously remain in your serene state whilst attending the course or book reading, it may well blow your socks off!

Which techniques come next?

You can learn as many techniques as you like, but this is working backwards. It is attempting to force your condition from the outside inwards. Doing what others advise is best for you.

The natural way is to activate dormant abilities when you don't desire, this works from the inside out, in response to what you really need.

Desiring skills and abilities rarely works because most of our desires are loaded with a feeling of 'I'm not ready yet'.

The real deal comes when you give yourself the freedom to mature in your own time from the inside outwards. We are all unique this cannot be prescribed.

Being what you have now.

It's all now

Spend increasing lengths of time acting out your divine character, until it becomes your very nature.

By giving yourself the space to spend more time in the serene self, you get back into the driving seat and take control of your own destiny.

There is no-longer a need to seek healing, it will follow naturally.

The path to enlightenment is now open and anticipating your next move.

Feel it, live it, being in the now.

Dream time

Now that you have access to your super intuition, use it, but don't become a slave to it. Always remain in balance.

Use your individuality and personality of the ego to do creative things. Create great desires that are sympathetic to your soul and the planet, in other words, create your target.
Then allow your spirit self to take you there, step by step. Don't worry about planning and detail, your spirit self will take care of that. Spirit and physical self team working in harmony.

Realise your dreams.

Ego focus upon the target

Spirit self guides you to the target

No limits

Connect your unlimited infinite divine inner self into the finite limited physical where it belongs.

Enjoy exploring and creating new possibilities

In the realm of Being there are no limits.

Limits only exist in the realm of thinking.

Zero point

This is the zero point of balance

The point of ultimate Love

The Love of Now

The no-thing of our true nature

You are no-thing and yet every-thing

Our immortal essence

Zero limits

Notes

I send heartfelt thanks to all my lovely friends and family who have helped create this book.

Further information about workshops, newsletters, forthcoming books and contact details can be found at www.nealedaniel.com

My books are currently available through Amazon and my printer lulu.com

Created in our garden shed using Inkflow.

Other books by Neale

Book one in the Love: Series

Love: Our Lost Story

If you are seeking your spiritual truth and have so far received unsatisfactory answers to your questions. This story provides an alternative explanation why spirituality on Earth is the way it is. This understanding could expand your consciousness in ways you are unlikely to have experienced before.

Our spiritual journey is presented to us as complicated, long and challenging, it does not have to be this way. There is a simple alternative approach; an approach hidden for thousands of years by false histories and legends, layer upon layer to hide the original truth.

The story takes you back to a time before history, religion and spiritual beliefs when humanity played a pure and simple divine spiritual role on Earth. It helps you to re-discover your birth right.

This is the story of humanity's love, it's creation, loss, and today it's rediscovery.